OPEN SESAME • Stage C
English as a Second Language Series

COOKIE MONSTER'S BLUE BOOK

Featuring Jim Henson's Sesame Street Muppets

Children's Television Workshop

Author

Jane S. Zion

Illustrators

Carolyn Bracken

Tom Brannon

Maggie Swanson

Jody Taylor

Photographer

Simon Baigelman

Oxford University Press

1985

Oxford University Press

200 Madison Avenue
New York, NY 10016 USA

Walton Street
Oxford OX2 6DP England

OXFORD is a trademark of
Oxford University Press.

Library of Congress Cataloging in
Publication Data

Zion, Jane S.
Cookie Monster's blue book.

(Open Sesame)
Summary: This third in a series of six
includes a student book, teacher's book,
activity book, and duplicating masters
for teaching English as a second
language to ages five to ten. Focuses on
the four skills: listening, speaking,
reading, and writing, using songs,
stories, conversations, games, etc.
1. English language—Text-books for
foreign speakers—Juvenile literature.
[1. English language—Textbooks for
foreign speakers] 1. Children's
Television Workshop. II. Title.
III. Series.
PE1128.Z55 1985 428.2′4 84-20753
ISBN 0-19-434158-5

The publisher would like to thank the
students and teachers of Public School
20 at 166 Essex Street, New York, New
York, for their participation in the
photography sessions for this book.

The publisher would like to thank Tom
Cooke for permission to reproduce *Meet
the Muppets*.

Developmental Editor: Debbie Sistino

Printing (last digit): 9

Printed in Hong Kong

PREFACE

Cookie Monster's Blue Book is for elementary school children learning English as a Second Language who already have some reading and writing ability in English. Vocabulary and grammar from the first two stages of the Open Sesame series are reintroduced and expanded so this stage can be a continuation or, for students new to the series, an entry level. Each of the lessons follows a carefully sequenced curriculum from topic to function to structure. The functions and structures are correlated with topics that are particularly suitable for children, such as the classroom, sports, and animals.

The focus is on all four skills. Children will develop their listening, speaking, reading, and writing skills through songs, chants, conversations, poems, stories, and games all based on illustrations and photographs in the book. By the end of the *Blue Book*, children are reading and writing at the short paragraph level and holding simple conversations. Visual cues at the top of each page indicate the purpose of each lesson.

Other components at this level include a Teacher's Book, an Activity Book, a Cassette, and Picture Cards.

 Song

 Chant or Poem

 Conversation between Muppets

 Share it Conversation between Children

 Story

 Activity

 Test

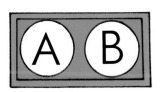 Test

 Review Test

CONTENTS

dining room

uncle

aunt

mother

grand-
father

father

living room

bathroom

kitchen

grandmother

brother

sister

bedroom

friend

3

- Where's your sister?
- What's she doing?

Greetings! My name is the Count
because I love to count!
I count everything I see.
Count, count, count with me!

1.

2.

3.

4.

5.

6.

hands

knees

legs

toes

arms

shoulders

2 big 👀, 1 little ⊙ ,

4 big 😁, 8 little 👣 ,

8 short 🖐🖐, long, long ,

2 big . They're a funny little pair!

left **right**

■ No, Ernie. Not your left arm, your right arm.

■ Sorry, Bert. I guess I made a mistake.

Hair

long
short
straight
curly
blond
red
black
brown

Eyes

brown
black
blue
green

- Do you have short hair?
- No, I don't.
- Do you have long hair?
- Yes, I do.

My friend is 7 years old.

Old toys are nice.
New toys are yucchy.
We have old toys.
Aren't we lucky!

1. wet hats

   dry hats

2. dirty pots

   clean pots

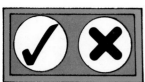

LISTENING TEST

1.

 ✓ ✗

2. ✓ ✗

3. ✓ ✗

4. ✓  ✗

5. ✓  ✗

6. ✓  ✗

7. ✓  ✗

8. ✓ 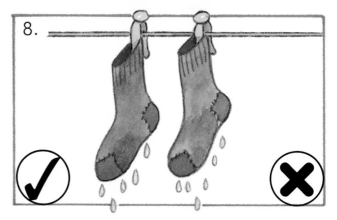 ✗

ruler

book

paste

3

pen

scissors

paints

pencil

bookbag

paper

eraser

markers

crayons

13

5¢
nickel

25¢
quarter

1¢
penny

10¢
dime

$1.00
dollar

■ Let's count by tens!

■ Let's count by fives!

14

■ How much are the pencils?
■ They're 15¢ each.

■ Where's my book?

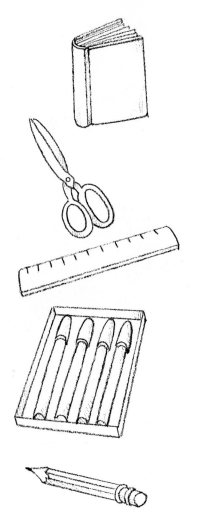

in

on

under

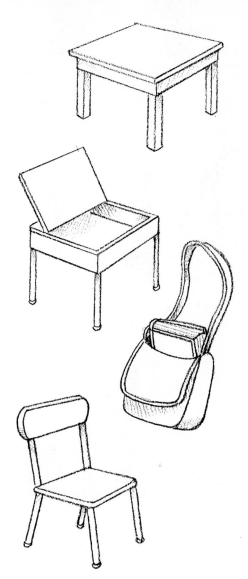

■ What time is it?
■ It's one o'clock.

1:00

2:30

3:00

4:30

5:00

6:30

7:00

8:30

9:00

10:30

11:00

12:30

17

- What time is it?
- It's nine o'clock.
- It's time for English.

math

social studies

science

music

LISTENING TEST

1.

2.

3.

4.

5.

6.

7

8.

4

After School Club ☆

Monday

He rides his bicycle.

She plays tennis.

Tuesday

He plays checkers.

He plays football.

Wednesday

She runs.

■ What does he do on Monday?

20

Thursday

Friday

He plays the guitar.

He paints pictures.

He dances.

She plays kickball.

She plays the piano.

■ What does she do on Monday?

21

It's Monday.
I bring my racket
with me.

It's Tuesday.
He brings his paints
with him.

It's Wednesday.
She brings her
sneakers with her.

It's Thursday.
We bring our guitars
with us.

It's Friday. They bring
their radios with them.

■ What do you want to do on Monday?

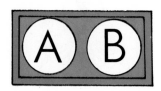 **LISTENING TEST**

Monday	Tuesday	Wednesday	Thursday	Friday

1. (A) Monday   (B) Tuesday
2. (A) Thursday   (B) Friday
3. (A) Monday   (B) Wednesday
4. (A) They dance.   (B) They play checkers.
5. (A) She rides her bicycle.   (B) She plays kickball.

1. It's a warm and rainy day.

2. It's a warm and windy day.

3. It's a hot and sunny day.

4. It's a cool and cloudy day.

5. It's a cold and snowy day.

Spring is here. Little are on the . is planting . will grow.  need and to grow.

Now it is summer. The on the are big and  .

 is watering her and .

They will grow big. The  are still very little.

Fall is here. The  on the are , ,
and . The are big now. will make
for Halloween. She will make for Thanksgiving.

Now it is winter. There are no on the . It is . is making . She will plant more in the spring. New will grow.

- What am I wearing?
- Are you wearing blue pants?
- Yes, I am.
- Are you wearing a red shirt?
- No, I'm not.

red   **blue**   yellow   **green**   **purple**

pink   **brown**   **black**   orange   **white**   **gray**

| shorts | pants | shoes | sneakers | blouse |
| shirt | sweater | skirt | dress | socks |

LISTENING TEST

1.

2.

3.

4.

5.

6.

7.

8.

6 LISTENING TEST

Pick A or B.

1.
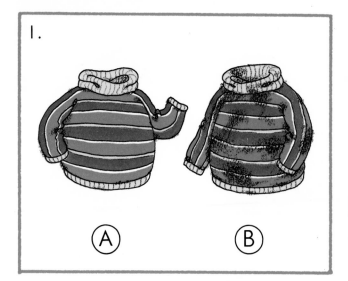

(A)   (B)

2.

(A)   (B)

3.
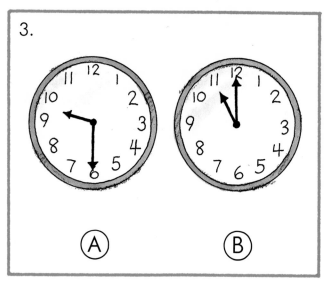

(A)   (B)

4.
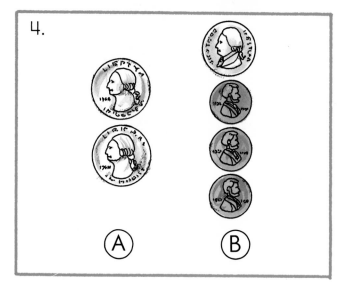

(A)   (B)

5.
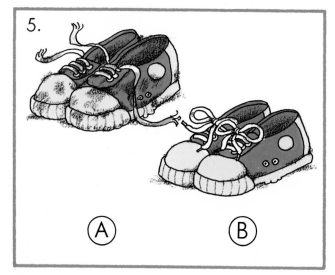

(A)   (B)

6.
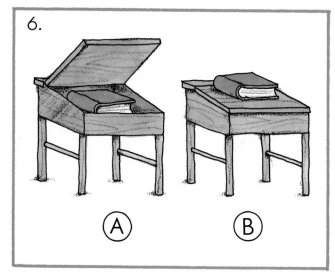

(A)   (B)

READING TEST

Pick A, B, or C.

1. (A) These are yellow pants.
   (B) This is a red skirt.
   (C) These are red pants.

2. (A) The crayons are under the chair.
   (B) The crayons are on the chair.
   (C) The markers are on the chair.

3. (A) His sister is in the kitchen.
   (B) His father is in the kitchen.
   (C) His sister is in the bathroom.

4. (A) It's 6:00.
   (B) It's 3:30.
   (C) It's 4:30.

5. (A) It's summer.
   (B) It's spring.
   (C) It's fall.

READING TEST

Pick A, B, or C.

1. This is Penny. She has black eyes and a red nose.
   She has short, brown hair.

2. He has three pencils. The pencils are yellow.
   The pencils are not on his chair.
   The pencils are not on his desk.
   The pencils are in his desk.

WRITING TEST

Tina is in the living room. She is watching TV. Her father is in the living room. He is reading a book.

What's the answer?
1. Who is in the living room?
2. Where is Tina?
3. What is her father doing?

It is spring. The birds are in the tree. Prairie Dawn is planting seeds. The seeds will grow into big pumpkins.

What's the question?
1. Who . . . ?
2. Where . . . ?
3. What . . . ?

WRITING TEST

What's the word?

WINTER FUN

It's a cold and [image] day. Ernie is playing in the snow.

He's wearing green [image] , a purple [image] , a [image]

jacket and [image] mittens. Ernie likes the winter!

THE AFTER SCHOOL CLUB

Rodeo Rosie likes the After School Club. On Monday, she [image] .

On Tuesday, she [image] . On Wednesday, she

plays the [image] . On Thursday, she plays [image] .

On Friday, she dances and listens to her [image] .

Just for Fun!

Let's all dance together!

7

chicken

steak

peanuts

fish

eggs

yogurt

milk

butter

cheese

ice cr

38

carrots

green beans

potatoes

oranges

pears

tomatoes

cereal

rice

spaghetti

cookies

bread

39

- May I have a fork?
- Here you are.
- No, not a knife, a fork!

| fork | spoon | napkin | plate |
| bowl | glass | cup | saucer |

What food group is it in?

START

Go ahead **1** space

Go back **2** spaces

Meat Group

Fruit and Vegetable Group

Milk Group

Grain Group

RICE

Meat Group

Fruit and Vegetable Group

Milk Group

Grain Group

Miss **1** turn

■ Let's make a salad. Do we have any lettuce?

■ Yes, we have one wonderful head of lettuce. Count it. One!

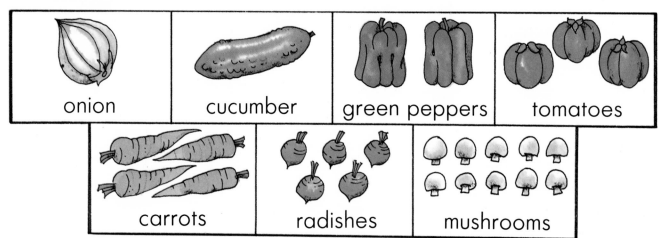

| onion | cucumber | green peppers | tomatoes |

| carrots | radishes | mushrooms |

LISTENING TEST

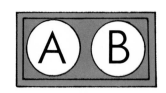

1. (A) Cookie Monster   (B) Prairie Dawn
2. (A) milk   (B) an apple
3. (A) a fork   (B) a knife
4. (A) in a glass   (B) in a saucer
5. (A) cheese   (B) chicken
6. (A) an apple   (B) spaghetti

doctor

dentist

bus driver

police officer

teacher

bank teller

fire fighter

mail carrier

mechanic

cashier

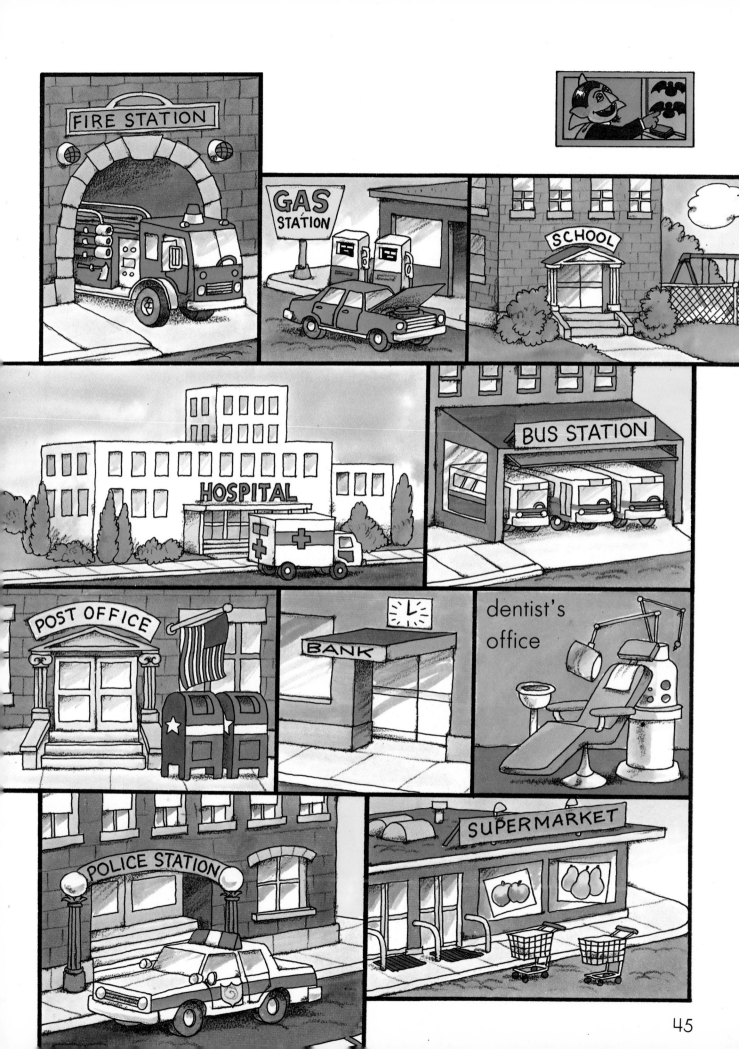

45

■ What do you want to be?

■ Do you want to be a dentist?

46

■ Where's the library?

■ It's on the right. It's across from the supermarket.

Every morning Bert gets up at 6:00.

He eats breakfast at 7:00.

Between 11:00 and 3:00 he helps people.

He gets to work and changes into his uniform at 9:00.

He listens to his radio and answers calls at 9:30.

Bert gets home and eats dinner at 5:30.

He goes to bed at 8:00.

LISTENING TEST

Farmer Grover's Farm

9

■ Where are all the animals?

Jungle World

■ Where are all the animals?

52

The Friendly Forest

■ Where are all the animals?

The Bird Who Couldn't Fly

1. I want to fly. Can you help me?

You don't have webbed feet. Try these.

2. But Big Bird still couldn't fly.

Oh, I can do that.

5. Oh no! How will I get my eggs back in the nest?

55

- What animal do you want to be? Why?
- Where will you live?
- What will you do?

1.

2.

3.

4.

5.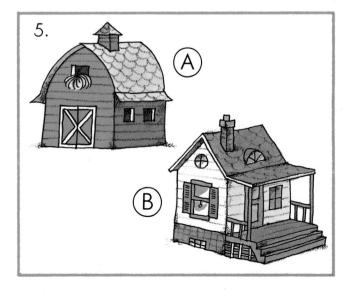

6.

10 My Feelings

Sometimes I'm angry.
Sometimes I'm not.

Sometimes I'm happy.
That happens a lot.

Sometimes I'm sad,
but that's O.K. with me.

Sometimes I'm surprised.
Do you feel that way too?

Sometimes I'm scared.
I don't like to be.

Sometimes I'm proud,
like when I'm with you.

So many feelings inside you see,
and I like these feelings because they're me!

59

Ernie's Sad Dream

3.

4.

6.

■ How do you feel about it?

LISTENING TEST

1.

2.

3.

4.

5.

6.

January

bus

February

car

May

train

June

sailboat

September

rowboat

October

motorcycle

March

bicycle

April

motorboat

July

helicopter

August

airplane

November

truck

December

horse

The Birthday Surprise

1. One day Grover was taking a birthday present to his mommy.

2. The bus hit a bump! The present landed on a boat.

5. Prairie Dawn took him to shore.

6. Rodeo Rosie took Grover home.

3. Grover followed the boat.

4. He finally got the present.

7. Goodbye, Rodeo Rosie.

8. Happy Birthday, Mommy!

Thank you, Grover. What a surprise! How was your trip?

■ Where do you want to go?

■ When do you want to go?

■ How do you want to go?

June

Sunday	Monday	Tuesday	Wednesday	Thursday	Friday	Saturday
1	2	3 contest	4	5	6	7
8	9	10	11	12	13 contest	14
15 convention	16	17	18	19	20	21 meeting
22 meeting	23	24	25	26	27	28
29	30					

- Hello, Bill's Barber Shop. Can I help you?
- Yes, please. I want to get my hair cut.
- How about Tuesday?
- Which Tuesday?
- Tuesday, June third.
- No, I can't. I have a chess contest.

LISTENING TEST

1. (A) Prairie Dawn   (B) Grover
2. (A) a car   (B) a motorcycle
3. (A) in March   (B) in July
4. (A) Ernie   (B) Herry Monster
5. (A) a car   (B) a train
6. (A) in September   (B) in August

LISTENING TEST

Pick A or B.

1.

2.

3.
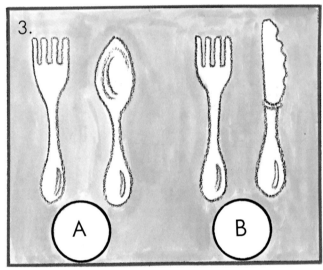

4.

5.
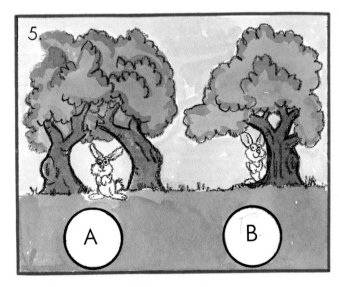

6.
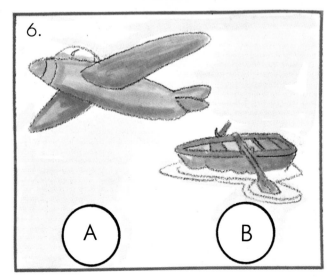

READING TEST

Pick A, B, or C.

1. Ⓐ The zebra is black and white.
   Ⓑ The skunk is black and white.
   Ⓒ The horse is black and white.

2. Ⓐ The supermarket is on the left.
   Ⓑ The post office is on the right.
   Ⓒ The supermarket is on the right.

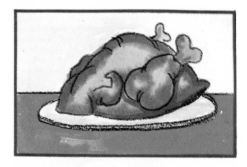

3. Ⓐ Chicken is from the meat group.
   Ⓑ Chicken is from the grain group.
   Ⓒ Chicken is from the milk group.

4. Ⓐ She is angry.
   Ⓑ She is sad.
   Ⓒ She is surprised.

5. Ⓐ The helicopter is in the water.
   Ⓑ The helicopter is in the air.
   Ⓒ The sailboat is in the air.

READING TEST

Pick A, B, or C.

1. This animal lives on the farm. It is brown and white.
   It is not in front of the farmhouse. It is between the
   farmhouse and the barn.

2. This food is from the fruit and vegetable group.
   It is a fruit. Its name is the same as its color.

WRITING TEST

Betty Lou wants to go to the library. She is asking
Bert how to get there. The library is to the left of
the hospital.

What's the answer?
1. Who wants to go to the library?
2. What is she doing?
3. Where is the library?

It is 7:00. It is time to milk the cows. Farmer Grover is in the barn.
He is milking the cows. He is happy. He likes to milk the cows.

What's the question?
1. Who . . . ?
2. What . . . ?
3. Where . . . ?

WRITING TEST

What's the word?

A WONDERFUL SALAD

Cookie Monster will make a wonderful !

What will he put in the salad? He has one head of

lettuce, two long, , one big,

 , three little green peppers and one big .

This salad will be good!

A LONG TRIP

Prairie Dawn went to see her friend last June.

The was hot. Her friend lives very far away

from Sesame Street. First, Prairie Dawn took an .

Then she took a  . After that she took a .

Her friend met her and they went home in a .

They had a wonderful time!

Just for Fun!

Clap your hands together!